ART OF PROTEST

CREATING, DISCOVERING, AND ACTIVATING ART FOR YOUR REVOLUTION

DE NICHOLS

ILLUSTRATED BY

**DIANA DAGADITA, SADDO, OLIVIA TWIST,
MOLLY MENDOZA, AND DIEGO BECAS**

BPP

"ART IS
IF YOU DON'T
EVERY

NOTHING REACH SEGMENT OF THE PEOPLE."

—KEITH HARING

CONTENTS

INTRODUCTION 8

01 WHY ART MATTERS IN SOCIAL MOVEMENTS

MY STORY AS AN ARTIVIST IN FERGUSON 10

THE *MIRROR CASKET* 12

WHY ART MATTERS IN SOCIAL MOVEMENTS 14

TRY THIS 16

02 WHAT EXACTLY IS PROTEST ART?

HOW I FIRST ENCOUNTERED PROTEST ART 18

DEFINING PROTEST ART 20

A BRIEF HISTORY 26

WHAT DO YOU SEE? (KEITH HARING) 30

SYMBOLISM 32

WHAT DO YOU SEE? (JACOB LAWRENCE) 34

COLOR 36

WHAT DO YOU SEE? (RAINBOW FLAG) 38

VISUAL VERSUS VERBAL LANGUAGE 40

TYPOGRAPHY 42

TRY THIS 44

03 YOUTH LEADERSHIP AND PROTEST ART AROUND THE WORLD

A VISIT TO SOUTH AFRICA   46
YOUTH-LED MOVEMENTS   48
SOUTH AFRICA   50
THE UMBRELLA MOVEMENT   52
THE STUDENTS OF PARKLAND   54
YOUNG CLIMATE ACTIVISTS   56
TRY THIS   62

04 PROTEST ART BEYOND TODAY

WHAT LIES AHEAD   64
TECHNOLOGY AND PROTEST ART   66
MICRO-PROTEST   70
TRY THIS   72
OVER TO YOU   74

MEET THE CREATORS   76
SOURCE NOTES AND IMAGE CREDITS   79

INTRODUCTION

When I was a kid growing up in Mississippi and Tennessee, I learned pretty early about social injustices that exist in the world.

I remember defending myself against bullies who did not like me because of my dark skin. I recall watching my favorite TV shows and learning about South African apartheid, police brutality, the global AIDS crisis, and historic movements for civil rights through episodes that dared to highlight these causes.

As I recognized the power of the media in expanding my knowledge, I began to create art in my teens that reflected the issues happening around me—9/11, Hurricane Katrina, the Jena Six trials. And by the time I found myself as an arts organizer on the ground in the 2014 Ferguson Uprising, I felt equipped with the experience to deploy art as a way of bringing people together to raise our collective voices.

Throughout this book, you will learn the art of protest through the many artworks, experiences, and campaigns that have been created across the world to protest social injustices and advocate for the rights and liberties of diverse communities. You will learn a bit of my story as well as the stories of others—leaders, artists, youth, and everyday people—who have used art as a tool for organizing communities and catalyzing change. However, I hope you will also learn the art of *protesting*. Tips and strategies are shared throughout this book to help you exercise creative ways to mindfully organize, create, and protest with others. Suggested art activities range from writing simple protest signs to designing banners, building sculptures, organizing flash mobs, and making cause-specific artworks.

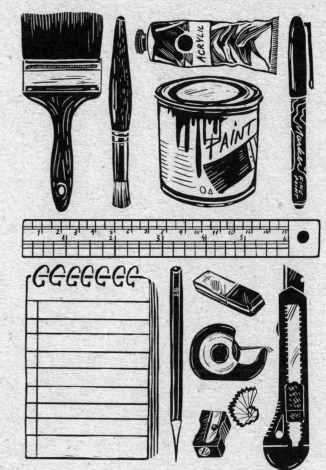

With this, you might be more compelled to raise your voice about the issues, causes, and global concerns that matter to you. Our society constantly experiences waves of social movements, campaigns for justice, and fights against climate issues and disease on a global scale. And no matter where you live, or what language you speak, or what cause you choose, it is my hope that this book will encourage and equip you to use art as a language and instrument that can help you champion your chosen cause.

01 WHY ART MATTERS IN SOCIAL MOVEMENTS

MY STORY AS AN ARTIVIST IN FERGUSON

On August 9, 2014, my life—like those of many in my home city of St. Louis, Missouri—was forever changed when I learned that a teenager had been killed by a police officer while walking along the streets of his grandmother's neighborhood. His name was Michael Brown Jr., and his body lay in the street for four and a half hours as news media captured photos and people crowded around in dismay. Over the days that followed, hundreds of people began to march in protest across the small municipality of Ferguson, Missouri, where he lived. I was one of them, and after daily— and soon nightly—protesting, I wanted to do something more.

At that time, I was an educator at our local contemporary art museum. I'd just finished graduate school in social work, and I'd been active as a community-based artist and designer in collaboration with schools, neighborhoods, and artists all across the region. In response to the Ferguson Uprising, I created a digital platform called Connected for Justice that helped allies donate and distribute resources to people on the ground. I also collaborated with a photographer to develop *Faces of the Movement*, a photographic series that dignified and amplified the stories of people involved in the uprising. And my best friend, Sophie, and I even went door-to-door across Ferguson recording *United Story*, a video series of stories featuring neighbors and families whose streets and homes became central to the growing protests. Others in our "artivists" collective created works that amplified movement slogans like "Hands Up, Don't Shoot," performed flash mobs, and placed guerrilla installations in public spaces to help spread the messages of the protests.

THE *MIRROR CASKET*

Of all the projects that the artivists and I created, we became most known for the *Mirror Casket.* This project emerged from a series of dreams I had after my first nights of protesting. Each dream included men walking into the night carrying a casket that was made of mirrors. I couldn't shake the image, so I reached out to as many artists as I knew to ask for help to bring it to life. Six artists responded, and in a matter of weeks, we worked together to gather materials, design the casket, build it, and march it from the street where Michael Brown Jr. was murdered to the police department where many had gathered nightly to protest.

After its first use, the *Mirror Casket* appeared in subsequent marches across the region and was exhibited throughout Missouri, including in the capitol. During the year that followed, it gained the attention of the Smithsonian Institution, which acquired it for its latest museum, the National Museum of African American History and Culture in Washington, DC. Activist Angela Davis even wrote an article about it for *Smithsonian* magazine, titled "The Art of Protest."

Eventually, the public awareness gained from the *Mirror Casket* project and other protest artworks allowed me to meet, connect, and work with dozens of artists to conceive and develop more creations, performances, videos, and even apparel that address women's rights, LGBTQ+ issues, racial inequity, climate justice, and education. Together we have used art to help grassroots groups and organizations lobby for policy changes and influence the ways in which our communities can thrive more equitably.

WHY ART MATTERS IN SOCIAL MOVEMENTS

Most art that is created in protest will not be acquired by museums, nor is this usually the goal of activists and artists working together. Most often, we aim to reflect and respond to the immediate causes that are grounded in our social movements. And whether used in a march, in a social media campaign, or as guerrilla art in a public space, protest art helps social movements inform the public of issues, challenge the status quo, convey collective goals and messaging, imagine a vision of change, and persuade others to take action.

Informing the Public

When used in public spaces, protest art serves as a mighty tool to help people learn about social issues. As an example, *Chalked Unarmed* was a guerrilla art series by public performance artist and *Mirror Casket* collaborator Mallory Nezam. The project invited citizen collaborators to create chalk outlines, like police outlines of murder victims, on sidewalks across their communities. Each outline was filled with the name, date, and location of a person who had been murdered by a police officer.

Making Messages Visible

In protests across the globe, people tend to write and illustrate their calls to action on cardboard, posters, or banners. At marches, where it can be hard for target audiences to hear each individual's voice, signage allows each person's message to be seen, and the results are often full of creativity and passion.

Imagining a Vision for Change

Protest art effectively helps people develop a language and create a vision for how outcomes in a community can be better. While projects like the *Mirror Casket* challenge viewers to look inward to see themselves differently and empathize with those whose lives have been lost, other works may propel people forward to imagine a new reality.

Influencing Action

Efforts like Decolonize This Place and Theater of the Oppressed use performances, flash mobs, and "spect-acting" (whereby a member of the audience also becomes part of the performance) to engage with people across the world and explore how justice and equality can become reality. Each experience that the artists facilitate is directly tied to demands for organizations and government leaders to change a policy, boycott unjust spaces, disinvest from harmful companies, or stop violent or inequitable public actions. For example, Theater of the Oppressed ran a performance in 2016 entitled *The Housing Circus*, based on the real life experiences of different individuals trying to receive housing benefits. Drawing from the perspectives of LGBTQ+ individuals and war veterans living in New York City, Theater of the Oppressed used this performance to suggest policy changes.

Challenging the Status Quo

One of the common impacts of protest art is to push against the norms and rules of society. Artists like Elizabeth Vega, Ai Weiwei, Banksy, and others have mastered using art as dissent. Such works often take existing materials and cultural artifacts and repurpose them, or they might remix messages from advertisements, buildings, monuments, news articles, or political documents in ways that point to their hypocrisy, outdated messages, or other flaws.

TRY THIS:

1. **Write a list of all the social issues that you know about.** From your list, circle two or three that matter most to you. Brainstorm how art might be used to protest your selected issues as well as how art might help spark solutions to address them.

2. **Organize an artivist team around a cause you care about.** One of the arts of protesting is to work in community and collaboration with others in order to raise your voices around a social cause. Who among your friends or family can you partner with to create art together? Who within your community has created protest art before? Make a list of people you know and reach out to them to share your ideas.

3. **Create a protest sign.** Write or draw a sketch of what your sign will say. Then gather materials around your home like markers and cardboard to create your sign.

4. **Use everyday materials like boxes** to build a sculpture that can be carried in marches, installed at different sites, or used in public to draw attention to a social issue.

16

AN ARTIST'S DUTY AS FAR AS I'M CONCERNED IS TO REFLECT THE TIMES...

Nina Simone

02 WHAT EXACTLY IS PROTEST ART?

How I First Encountered Protest Art

Before I cocreated works like the *Mirror Casket*, my understanding of protest art had come from artifacts I saw in my hometown's civil rights museum. I spent my childhood in rural Mississippi, and then my family moved to Memphis, Tennessee, which is where Dr. Martin Luther King Jr. was assassinated in 1968 by a white supremacist, James Earl Ray, on the balcony of the Lorraine Motel. The Lorraine Motel was transformed into the National Civil Rights Museum in 1991 to memorialize the scene of Dr. King's murder and honor the work of the civil rights movement of the 1960s.

Dr. King had been in Memphis to speak in support of sanitation workers who were striking for fair wages and safer working conditions after two trash handlers were killed by a malfunctioning garbage truck. One of the works of art that became iconic of the strikes and labor marches was the "I Am a Man" poster, which was the brainchild of activists and union officials. After the riots and protests that erupted nationwide following Dr. King's death, "I Am a Man" posters continued to be used alongside posters that read "Honor King: End Racism!" These posters helped urge people to see the humanity and dignity of Black Americans.

Simultaneously, numerous social movements were happening in the United States and across the world, including the student movement, the anti-Vietnam War movement, the women's movement, the gay rights movement, and the environmental movement. Extending through the 1980s and into the 2000s, uprisings like the Arab Spring, Occupy Wall Street, and other cultural revolutions continued across the world, and protest art was front and center as an anchoring device for messaging and movement building. This chapter will take a look at some of these protests and the art they generated in more detail.

DEFINING PROTEST ART

To protest means to object to something. Protest art is a visual means of expressing that objection. It is often created and used collectively to inform others about a social issue, declare public objection to the issue, and persuade others to join in action to address it.

Protest art is one of many types of art forms used for activism. Activism involves efforts that "promote, impede, direct, or intervene in social, political, economic, or environmental reform with the desire to make changes in society." Artistic activism—or as I like to call it, artivism—combines activism with the creative power of visual, performative, and experiential art in order to seek positive change. In addition to protest art, artivism can include:

Craftivism

"Craftivism" encompasses a variety of do-it-yourself activities such as quilting, origami, and yarn bombing, which can be used to bring awareness to issues in public spaces.

In protests in Hong Kong, youth organizers have created thousands of origami cranes as a nonviolent symbol of their defiance and expression of their desire for democracy. Making cranes became an accessible way for people around the world to show solidarity with the protesters.

Street Art

Created for the purpose of public visibility, street art is a key outlet for protest artists and encompasses murals, graffiti, stickering, guerrilla art, flash mobs, and other performances. Street art offers an array of canvases and venues for expression, including public buildings, civic structures, and open land.

Tatyana Fazlalizadeh is an artist who created the Stop Telling Women to Smile project in protest of the street harassment that women are commonly subjected to in public. By protesting these behaviors in the places where they frequently occur—along sidewalks, near construction sites, outside of bars and restaurants—Fazlalizadeh illustrates the faces and stories of women who have experienced harassment in order to depict how widespread the problem is and to give a collective voice to the issue.

Michelle Angela Ortiz, a Latinx muralist, has created works like *Orgullo Otomi* and *Familias Separadas* that have been exhibited in Costa Rica, Ecuador, Mexico, Argentina, Spain, Venezuela, Honduras, and Cuba. Her work often portrays the stories of women, children, and families and the challenges and victories they face throughout their respective countries as well as those encountered in migration.

Guerrilla Art

Grounded in anonymity, guerrilla art is a type of street art that began in the UK. It is employed to visually express ironic or bold political messages, and thus it often takes form in unauthorized public spaces with the use of stickers, graffiti, sidewalk chalk, zines, or temporary sculptures.

Groups like the Guerrilla Girls wear masks as they produce performances and public art that bring attention to sexism and racism in the art world. The UK artist Banksy uses street art and murals to make satirical commentary on social issues, injustices, and political topics.

Public Performance

From flash dance mobs to playback theater and musical performances in the public square, performance art is one of the more accessible outlets for protest. It requires minimal materials, and with strong organizing (and sometimes choreography), it can easily scale from one person to hundreds, depending on the type of performance.

Die-ins (or lie-ins) are a popular form of public performance stemming from the sit-in direct actions that became popular during the civil rights movement of the 1960s. In sit-ins, protesters of racial injustice would occupy the seats of buses, restaurants, and other public spaces in order to disrupt operations until the movement's demands were met. Die-ins extend this concept by organizing people to lie on the ground—whether in malls, street intersections, or parks—in order to recognize those who have been affected by issues such as human trafficking, police brutality, violence, environmental injustice, and animal rights.

A powerful variation of a lie-in was led by American disability rights activists in the 1990s. As they advocated for the passing of the Americans with Disabilities Act (ADA) in the US Capitol, more than sixty protesters abandoned their wheelchairs, crutches, and helpers to crawl up the steps of the building. This demonstration by the Capitol Crawlers amplified the need for policy that would end discrimination and segregation of people with mental and physical disabilities as well as to ensure that public spaces are equipped with the amenities for their fair and equal access and treatment.

Projection Art

Using photography, video, graphic design, and technology, artists increasingly project their messages for change on surfaces and walls in public spaces. During the 2020 racial protests in the United States, federal building walls, architectural façades, and monument plinths became key canvases that rendered the demands of protesters visual and memorialized the victims of police brutality. One of the artists most known for using projection art for protest is Polish industrial designer Krzysztof Wodiczko. He was an infant during the Warsaw Ghetto Uprising against Nazis in his home country, and his work has covered topics of war, religious conflict, immigration, and cultural trauma in more than eighty spaces across the world.

Political Art

Sometimes finding protest art is as easy as opening your newspaper. Political cartoons and illustrations have been a primary tool for speaking about unfair policies and corruption since before the creation of printed publications. Political art often uses caricature, satire, and irony to express its critiques. Because their depictions can cause great public embarrassment to their targets, political artists often face lawsuits and ridicule. Syrian artist Ali Ferzat is considered one of the most influential and well-known political artists of the Middle East and has had over 15,000 caricatures and satirical drawings published. Following the publication of several anti-government cartoons in 2011, Ferzat was attacked and forced to live in exile.

Culture Jamming

Culture jamming is a type of protest that disrupts mass media and consumer culture by remixing the visuals, words, and platforms of advertising. It is also called "subvertising" and is one of the most striking forms of protest because of how it lures viewers in with expectations of familiar content, then unsettles them with its provocative messages. Some examples of culture jamming include doppelgänger branding, flash mobs, and hacktivism. During the 2020 US presidential election, designers placed the names of Black Americans who had been murdered by police on election signs outside the White House. Some signs declared "Vote for Breonna Taylor," a young Black medical worker who was shot and killed during a botched police raid. The signs were created by the Courageous Conversation Global Foundation as part of a campaign called "Vote for Them."

Photography

The power of a photo can change the public's perception of protest, which makes the role of photojournalists, novice documentarians, and even vloggers so critical. Black teenager Michael Brown had his hands up when he was killed by police in Ferguson, Missouri, in 2014. In the aftermath of Brown's death, St. Louis–based artist Damon Davis took photographs of Ferguson residents' raised hands and placed them in store windows, a powerful installation that came to be called *All Hands On Deck*. In creating this work, Davis portrayed a sense of solidarity among the community. Some images from the project are shown on the opposite page.

Poetry

Protest poetry addresses world issues and injustices through lyrical expression—both written and spoken. One powerful example is June Jordan's searing poem "A Song for Soweto," which appears on the next page. Poems can use a range of wordplay and rhetorical techniques, including repetition, internal and end-line rhyme, puns, and metaphor, to engage readers. And spoken word poetry adds the power of performance to command attention, impart emotion, and inspire action. Because of its powers, poetry fuels moments of resistance and has often served as a grounding art form for social movements.

Music

Like poetry, music defines cultures, eras, and moments in time. In social movements across the world, musicians and activists have created everything from hymns to chants to mainstream pop hits to reflect the energy and voices of people in protest. In the United States, spiritual and protest songs were an essential source of both sustenance and messaging during the civil rights movement of the 1960s. In some countries, music has served as such a powerful force for change, storytelling, and direction that governments felt the need to censor or ban certain songs or music.

"A Song for Soweto" by June Jordan

At the throat of Soweto
  a devil language falls
  slashing
    claw syllables to shred and leave
    raw
      the tongue of the young
        girl
          learning to sing
          her own name

Where she would say
        water
They would teach her to cry
        blood
Where she would save
        grass
They would teach her to crave
        crawling into the
          grave
Where she would praise
        father
They would teach her to pray
        somebody please
        do not take him
          away
Where she would kiss with her mouth
        my homeland
They would teach her to swallow
        this dust
But words live in the spirit of her face and that
sound will no longer yield to imperial erase

Where they would draw
        blood
She will drink
        water
Where they would deepen
        the grave
She will conjure up
        grass
Where they would take
        father and family away
She will stand
        under the sun/she will stay
Where they would teach her to swallow
        this dust
She will kiss with her mouth
        my homeland

and stay
with the song of Soweto

stay
with the song of Soweto

A BRIEF HISTORY

Protest art has been a "visual voice" for communities throughout history.

Political satire has been used as far back as ancient Greece and Rome and perhaps even earlier. Ancient Egyptian artwork depicted men as animals, while sculptors in the Middle Ages carved humorous scenes into stone. Exaggerated plays and public performances to express dissent about political and social issues are also well-documented. In the 1800s and early 1900s, protest art took the form of etchings, satirical cartoons, and publication covers; the last two categories are still useful strategies today.

Here's a look at the use of various art forms in protests of the modern era. This time line is representative but far from complete. What other instances of protest art through history and in the current day would you add?

1810–1820
Francisco Goya, Spain
THE DISASTERS OF WAR

This series of eighty-two politically charged etchings shows wartime scenes. Although the etchings were not published in Goya's lifetime, today they are seen as powerful indictments of the horrors of war.

1916
Dada Artists, Europe
ART AGAINST WORLD WAR I

Led by revolutionary icons including Marcel Duchamp and Man Ray, the Dadaists voiced an artistic revolt against conventional society and war via performance pieces, sculpture, poetry, and paintings.

1914–1918
Women's Suffrage Groups, UK
VOTES FOR WOMEN

Between 1914 and 1918, an estimated 2 million women in the UK undertook roles that had traditionally been filled by men, as most men of age had gone off to fight in World War I. This helped spur women to demand the right to vote, and new printing techniques enabled the activists to spread their messages quickly via posters, sashes, badges, and banners. British women gained the vote in 1918.

1920s–1930s
NAACP, USA
"A MAN WAS LYNCHED YESTERDAY"

A flag bearing these words was hung from the headquarters of the National Association for the Advancement of Colored People in order to raise awareness about the lynching of Black people in the United States. It was flown on multiple occasions until the building's landlords threatened the NAACP with eviction.

1920s
Diego Rivera, Mexico
MURALS

Rivera was a leader in a government-sponsored Mexican mural project that ran during the 1920s. His large-scale works centered around political and social themes that reflected on Mexico's history.

1929
Igbo Women, Nigeria
THE WOMEN'S WAR

In what is known as the "Aba Women's Riots of 1929," thousands of Igbo women took action against British colonial authorities who planned to impose a tax on market workers that endangered their livelihood. Messages initially spread through the community via palm leaves, which symbolized a call for help. The women then began performing nightly chants, songs, and dances, forcing some local chiefs to resign. The Women's War became a historic example of feminist and anti-colonial protest in Nigeria.

1944
Tōyō Miyatake, USA
PHOTOGRAPHY

Japanese American photographer Miyatake captured the story of the imprisonment of Japanese Americans in internment camps during World War II through a series of poignant and powerful photographs.

1960s
Rev. Dr. Martin Luther King Jr., USA
CIVIL RIGHTS SPEECHES

Led by the Rev. Dr. Martin Luther King Jr. and others, the American civil rights movement sought to end racial discrimination and grant Black Americans equal rights by law. Dr. King's iconic speeches helped inspire and bring attention to the movement.

1960s–1970s
Emory Douglas, USA
BLACK PANTHER GRAPHICS

American artist Emory Douglas created many of the famous graphic works associated with the *Black Panther* newspaper, including the "All Power to the People" poster.

1960s–1970s
Anti-War Protests, USA
SLOGANS AND SONGS

The escalating US involvement in the Vietnam War led to increasing protests. Original folk songs became important expressions of anti-war sentiment, as did slogans such as "Make Love, Not War."

1975
Shigeo Fukuda, Poland
"VICTORY 1945"

Shigeo Fukuda was a multitalented artist. Among his works are several important protest images, including "Victory 1945," which depicts, in stark graphic style, an artillery shell apparently returning into a cannon barrel, a simple and affecting plea for an end to wars.

1987
June Struggle, South Korea
WORKERS' MARCHES

Throughout the month of June democratic protests broke out, leading to reforms that are still in place in the South Korean government today. Originally started by students, and later joined by white-collar workers, the movement included throwing toilet paper rolls in the streets.

1990s
Piss on Pity, UK
THE DISABILITY ARTS MOVEMENT

The disability arts movement became active in the UK during the 1990s. The provocative slogan "Piss on Pity," coined by songwriter and activist Alan Holdsworth, was a rallying cry. The movement's activism led to the passing of the 1995 Disability Discrimination Act.

2010–2012
The Arab Spring
SOCIAL MEDIA

This series of anti-government demonstrations from Egypt to Tunisia, Syria, and beyond led to some changes in regime. Helped by social media, the pro-democratic movement spread quickly.

2015–2016
Anti-Government Protests, Brazil
PIXULECOS

After allegations of government corruption and in an unstable economy, millions of Brazilians took part in anti-government protests across the country, resulting in the successful impeachment of its president. Men, women, and children wore the vibrant yellow T-shirts of the national soccer team and passed inflatable dolls that caricatured corrupt politicians called "Pixulecos" through the crowds.

2018
Pascal Boyart, Paris
GILETS JAUNES MURAL

In 2018, the street artist Boyart painted a mural in Paris celebrating the "yellow vest" anti-government protests. It was based on a painting by Eugène Delacroix, *Liberty Leading the People*, which glorified the French revolution of 1830.

2020
Black Lives Matter, Global
STREET ACTIONS

Founded in 2013 by Alicia Garza, Patrisse Cullors, and Opal Tometi, the Black Lives Matter movement received international attention in 2020 following the unlawful killing of George Floyd, an unarmed Black man, at the hands of the police. Floyd's calls for help were repeated across the world, summarized by the phrase "I Can't Breathe."

WHAT DO YOU SEE?

Sometimes a visual style can become strongly associated with certain social movements. The artist Keith Haring had a distinctively bold and graphic visual style, and his work often reflected social issues, particularly the AIDS crisis. Even after his death from AIDS-related complications in 1990, his art continues to raise awareness.

In his piece *Ignorance = Fear*, Haring took influence from the ancient Japanese pictorial maxim "See no evil, hear no evil, speak no evil," which is traditionally depicted with three wise monkeys. Haring repurposed this maxim to reflect on how he felt about the US government's failure to act on the AIDS crisis.

Inverted Pink Triangle
This flipped version of the symbol used to identify gay men in Nazi camps is used here as a symbol of proud self-identification.

Pink *X*'s
Symbolizing death, these crosses represent the AIDS disease and the danger it poses to people ignorant about its spread and symptoms.

The Human
Haring's bold, highly stylized human forms allow for universal empathy.

Equal Sign (=)
Using the = symbol instead of the written word *equals* delivers the message faster while also presenting the statement as mathematical fact.

Red and Yellow
These two colors are associated with danger and fear in nature. Haring uses both for his figures here.

SYMBOLISM

Protest art often makes use of symbols, which can quickly convey powerful meaning.

Paper Cranes

In Japan, it is believed that someone who folds 1,000 origami cranes will be granted a wish. In 1945, two-year-old Sadako Sasaki was in the vicinity of the atomic bomb dropped on Hiroshima. She suffered long-term effects from that exposure, including developing leukemia. Before she died at the age of twelve, Sadako folded more than 1,000 cranes, and the paper crane went on to become a symbol of peace.

The Peace Sign

The peace sign was created by the British artist Gerald Holtom in 1958 as the logo for a campaign for nuclear disarmament in the UK. It has since become an iconic symbol of calls for peace.

Umbrellas

During protests for democracy in Hong Kong in 2014, activists used umbrellas as shields against tear gas and other aggressions by the police. The umbrellas came to symbolize the protests and gave the movement its name (read more on pages 52–53).

The Clenched Fist

The image of an upraised clenched fist is a powerful symbol of protest and resistance. Some of its first uses were by labor unions in the early 1900s, before it grew in popularity and became a symbol of many causes, including Black Power, the anti-apartheid movement, and the feminist movement.

The Rainbow

The rainbow is the most iconic symbol of the LGBTQ+ movement. It represents diversity, acceptance, and the spectrum of human sexualities and genders.

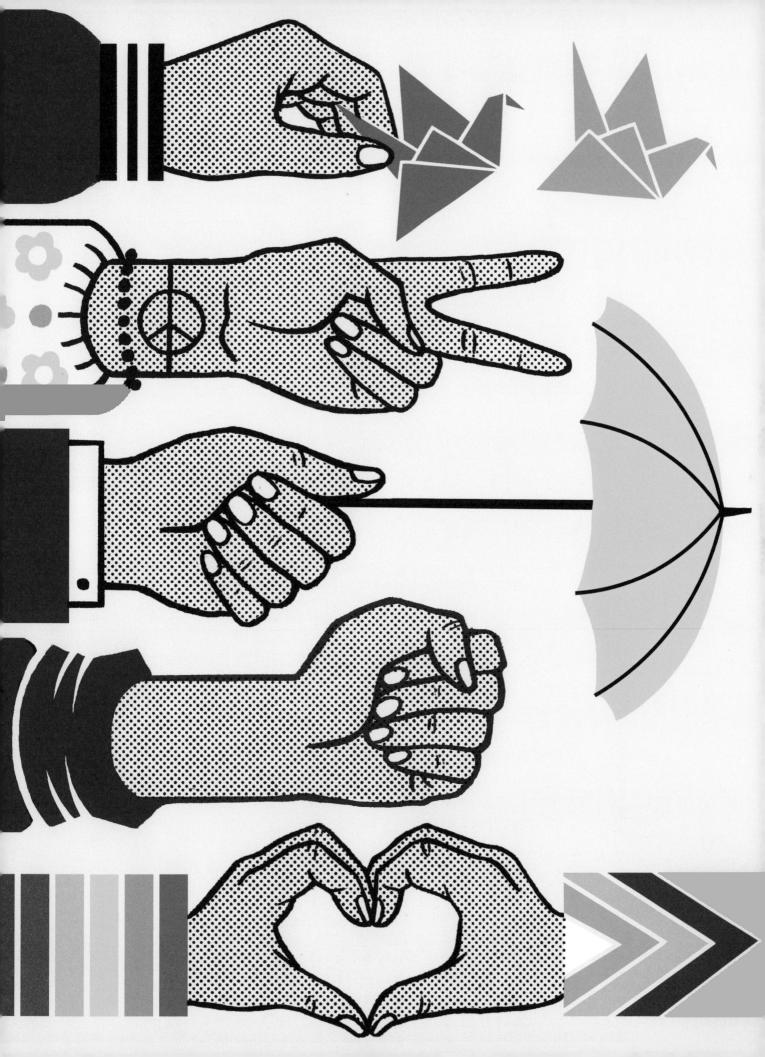

WHAT DO YOU SEE?

Artist Jacob Lawrence is known for his modernist depictions of African American history. He moved to Harlem in 1930, and many of his works feature the neighborhood he called home and its rich culture. Lawrence is recognized for his vibrant colors and blocky shapes, as well as expressive postures and faces. His artwork often has a narrative element, telling the stories of the struggles his community faced.

The 1948 painting *Ambulance Call* (shown on the opposite page) takes place on the streets of Harlem and portrays a medical emergency. At the heart of the image, a person lies on a stretcher carried by two attendants dressed in blue. At the time this image was painted, few hospitals in New York admitted Black patients, and consequently it took a long time for medical aid to arrive.

When you look closely at this painting, what do you see? How does the image make you feel, and why does it make you feel that way? Some of the imagery used in this work is explained in more detail below.

The Patient
In contrast to the figures looking down, the patient faces up at the crowd, perhaps suggesting a final farewell.

The Attendants
In 1948, it was rare for African Americans to be working in hospitals. The fact that Lawrence chooses three Black figures to represent the attendants and paramedic could indicate his acknowledgment that some advancements had been made in addressing systemic racism.

The Onlookers
With their heads positioned closely to one another, Lawrence shows a tight-knit community. Their down-turned mouths and eyes signify sadness, but perhaps they are seeking comfort in one another. Their grief seems to be in contrast to the bright primary colors Lawrence uses, suggesting hope and perseverance.

COLOR

Color is an essential aspect of any visual artwork. Different colors tend to evoke different moods, energies, or feelings, and protest art has utilized these properties to gain attention, support content, and drive action.

The Umbrella Movement—Hong Kong

Yellow
Happiness, positivity, joy, and warmth all come to mind when we think of the color yellow. However, it can also represent sickness, caution, and social ills.

Orange
The color orange can depict a range of concepts and emotions—from joy, fun, and creativity to health, stimulation, irritation, and caution.

Orange Revolution—Ukraine

LGBTQ+ movement—Universal

Purple
Historically, purple dye was very expensive and difficult to source, so the color tended to be reserved for royalty. In modern times, purple is associated with courage, ambition, wisdom, peace, and relaxation, as well as the LGBTQ+ movement.

Black
Black can connote a wide range of qualities, from mystery and darkness to despair, strength, and sophistication. Because black was one of the first colors used in art, its versatility is boundless and timeless—from the charcoal that prehistoric artists used to draw to the felt pens, paints, and digital prints found in protests around the world.

Black Panther movement—US

Pink

Bright-pink pigments have been found in prehistoric shale in the Sahara, thought to be from ancient organisms. Pink is sometimes associated with the feminine and has been used in the fights against period poverty. Animal rights activists have also used pink in protests against meat eating.

Women's suffrage—UK/US

Green

Green is one of the oldest and most common hues in nature as well as in art. It can represent money, success, freshness, harmony, growth, illness, decay, and more.

Abortion rights—Argentina

Indigo Revolt—India

Blue

Blue is one of the most popular hues used across contemporary societies. It is the color of the two largest features of nature—the sky and water—but different pigments such as YInMn are still being discovered to this day.

White

White often represents purity, innocence, safety, cleanliness, life, and death. White paint made from lead, which is highly toxic, was used by artists for hundreds of years before it was banned in the late twentieth century.

Red

Red can represent passion, love, life, anger, fire, power, and sacrifice. Because of its versatility, red was one of the first colors to be broken down into different shades and used in art.

SEX

LIFE

HEALING

SUNLIGHT

NATURE

MAGIC

SERENITY

SPIRIT

WHAT DO YOU SEE?

Artist and activist Gilbert Baker is credited with creating the first LGBTQ+ rainbow flag in 1978. The colors he chose represented the diversity of his community. The first rainbow flag had eight colored stripes that Baker dyed and stitched himself. Since some of the colors he chose were not widely available at the time, meaning the flag could not be mass-produced, his initial color choices underwent several revisions.

Less than a year later, Harvey Milk, the first openly gay elected politician in San Francisco, was assassinated. The Pride Parade Committee of 1979 removed the indigo stripe so that the flag's colors could be evenly divided along the procession route—with three colors on either side of the street. The six-striped flag remained the most widely used pride flag for decades.

Forty years after Baker's flag was designed, Daniel Quasar created the Progress Pride flag, which adds a chevron with black, brown, pink, blue, and white stripes to reaffirm the inclusion of people of color and transgender people in the LGBTQ+ movement.

What do these colors say to you? If you were to design your own flag, which colors would you use?

VISUAL VERSUS VERBAL LANGUAGE

In protest, artists communicate through both verbal and visual language. Verbal language includes speaking and writing, while visual language utilizes imagery, symbols, body language, motions, and other ways that we represent or communicate ideas visually. Even how we write our words can be visual language. Here are some of the ways that visual and verbal language intersect.

COLLAGE

Collage is the art of assembling parts of existing resources—whether magazines, books, maps, photographs, or other printed material—in order to make a new creation altogether. Photomontage is handy for conveying the magnitude of a cause or even portraying the many facets of an issue. In typography, collaging the letters or text from newspaper headlines, written policies, or other sources can help create emphasis on certain words or shine a light on how official statements contrast with reality.

HAND-WRITING

WHEN WE THINK ABOUT SCENES OF PROTEST, HAND-DRAWN SIGNS AND BANNERS ARE USUALLY THE MOST ASSOCIATED VISUALS—WHETHER IT'S A FELT PEN ON CARDBOARD OR MARKERS ON A POSTER BOARD.

THESE SIGNS ADD A PERSONAL FEELING TO THE MASSES OF PEOPLE, WHICH HELPS TO SHOW THAT AN EFFORT IS GRASSROOTS AND CONNECTED TO INDIVIDUALS' EXPERIENCES AND PERSPECTIVES.

SCREEN PRINTING AND LETTERPRESS

Screen printing is a printmaking technique that allows for mass production. Letterpress is a type of printmaking that entails paper being pressed over a raised bed of movable type that has been inked. In protest, screen printing, letterpress, and other printmaking forms such as etching, engraving, and woodcuts can transform chants, catchphrases, and graphic imagery into powerful protest art.

Digital Printing

Digitally designed and printed signs, banners, and other forms of protest communications can be used to emphasize a more formal or official tone to a protest.

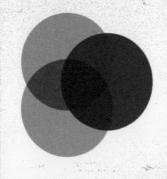

TYPOGRAPHY

Typography is the art of designing and arranging letters, words, and text in ways that appeal to viewers creatively. It includes the selection of fonts and styles, the sizes and shapes of letterforms, the arrangement of words and sentences, and even the spacing of characters and text. Typography is one way to use our understanding of verbal and visual language to express emotions and ideas in protest. And within typography, there are endless possibilities and considerations for how different techniques and styles can be used.

SERIF

Serifs are the short lines used in some typefaces at the end of letter strokes. Serif typefaces are most commonly used in paragraph form and can convey a scholarly, refined, or formal tone in visual language.

SLAB SERIF

Slab serif fonts are distinctive from other typefaces because of their blocky, flat, and thicker serifs. They are typically used for display type with the intention of grabbing a viewer's attention.

SANS SERIF

The term "sans serif" refers to typefaces without serifs. Sans serif fonts have a modern, streamlined look and are usually used in headlines or headings or to emphasize a declarative statement or a demand. Condensed sans serif fonts are usually bolded and set in all capital letters to intensify the most important statements or calls to action.

ALL CAPS

WORDS WRITTEN IN ALL CAPS CONVEY A **BOLDNESS** AND **POWER** SUGGESTING THAT THE MESSAGE IS BEING YELLED OR SHOUTED.

lowercase

text that is all in lowercase can suggest can suggest a youthful voice. it can also convey humility or lightheartedness or even be used to subvert more authoritarian tones.

TRY THIS:

1. **Learn about the history of protest art in your community or country.** Discover if there is a museum, gallery, or public space that honors the events that have happened in your hometown. Visit and explore any artworks that were created as part of a march, protest, or social movement. Note what features stand out in the art, and reflect on how these might inspire your creativity.

2. **Design a poster, using only words.** Protest art like the "I Am a Man" poster expresses a mantra—a slogan or phrase that is repeated to affirm a quality or state of being. Think about a statement, mantra, or quote that represents a social issue you care about. Draw it onto a large sheet of paper as a poster and get creative.

3. **Try making a banner.** Banners are a fun way to scale up the size and creativity of your protest messaging. Glue felt fabric to a bedsheet, stitch T-shirts together into a quilt, or use a long roll of butcher paper to make a banner that you and others might carry in support of your cause.

4. **Make a playlist of songs that inspire you to work for social change.** Be sure to include music from different genres and languages. Pay attention to the lyrics to understand the stories, topics, and calls to action that they express. To make it a collective effort, share your playlist with your friends and invite them to contribute.

WE CAN DO IT

"EVERYTHING IS ART. EVERYTHING IS POLITICS."

AI WEIWEI

03 YOUTH LEADERSHIP AND PROTEST ART AROUND THE WORLD

A VISIT TO SOUTH AFRICA

I got the chance to visit the home of former South African president Nelson Mandela during a solo adventure to Africa a few years ago. Upon visiting the Apartheid Museum, which chronicles the history of ending apartheid rule in the nation, I was struck by the ways that art and graphics had influenced the social movement, and also by the stories of youth leadership that had propelled the nation toward freedom. Having witnessed the vision and power of youth voices first-hand at the Ferguson Uprising, this visit made me want to learn more about how young people worldwide have led social movements.

YOUTH-LED MOVEMENTS

From Civil Rights to Black Lives Matter

John Lewis was a teenager when he began to dedicate his life to the struggle for racial equality in the United States. As a young man, he worked as a leader of the Student Nonviolent Coordinating Committee (SNCC), joining with other young people who put themselves on the line in the fight for desegregation in the South. In 1965, he was among the marchers badly beaten by police officers at the Edmund Pettus Bridge in Selma, Alabama. He went on to serve as a representative in Congress for his home state of Georgia for thirty-three years, from 1987 until his death in 2020, and remained a tireless fighter for racial justice throughout his life.

SOUTH AFRICA

In the mid-twentieth century, the Dutch and English colonial powers in South Africa imposed a stringent system of racial segregation known as apartheid. Students played a key role in protesting the segregation of the educational system, including restrictions against the use of their own languages in school in favor of English and the Dutch variant Afrikaans.

In June 1976, an estimated 200,000 schoolchildren took to the streets of Soweto, a township in Johannesburg, in protest. Twenty-five people were killed in the first days of the demonstrations, and as many as six hundred had died by the time the uprising was over. Many of those killed were children. The protest, and the brutal backlash against it, spoke to the national, then international, conscience and helped lead to the eventual end of apartheid.

To this day, South African teens are still protesting racism in their schools. In 2016, when she was thirteen years old, Zulaikha Patel led a protest at her school, which claimed that her natural hair violated its strict dress codes. Her leadership inspired further policy changes and movements, and the BBC named her one of its youngest celebrated global leaders.

MY HAIR DOESN'T NEED FIXING

2016

MY HAIR IS MY CHOICE

THE UMBRELLA MOVEMENT

After being held as a British territory for a century, Hong Kong was returned to Chinese rule in 1997. Although the territory was meant to maintain its autonomy, a series of restrictions on democratic processes followed. In 2014, a process was imposed that restricted candidates for office to those who had been screened by Chinese authorities.

In response, university students led a strike and a series of protests. They practiced civil disobedience by staging sit-ins at government buildings and by marching in public squares and streets, often banging pots and pans.

Protesters carried umbrellas to shield themselves from tear gas and other aggressive police tactics, and the umbrellas became a symbol of their resistance, a name for their movement, and a basis of their protest art. They wrote messages on umbrellas, placed them in the hands of public statues, created canopies of umbrellas that had been broken by police, and used them in other public installations.

The initial wave of protests lasted for seventy-nine days. A second wave began in 2019 in protest against a new law allowing the Hong Kong government to send suspected activists to mainland China to face trial. The student-led resistance has been severely quashed but carries on.

THE STUDENTS OF PARKLAND

Throughout recent decades, mass shootings have become a tragic and deadly epidemic in the United States, often affecting young people who are victimized by shootings within their schools.

In 2018, a student gunman killed seventeen people and injured seventeen more at the Marjory Stoneman Douglas High School in Parkland, Florida, the second deadliest school shooting in US history.

Student survivors of the shooting immediately became passionate and outspoken advocates for the reduction of gun violence. They sparked the Never Again campaign and led the national March for Our Lives, with more than 500,000 people gathering in Washington, DC, and more joining gatherings around the country. They also organized the Enough! National School Walkout Day, where students from three thousand schools nationwide left their classes for seventeen minutes to honor the lives of the seventeen people killed in Parkland. The March for Our Lives team continues to organize young people in America to own and use their collective power to fight against gun violence.

ENOUGH

PROTECT KIDS NOT GUNS

YOUNG CLIMATE ACTIVISTS

The number of young activists across the world is rising. Their collective work has been described as the most remarkable and important mass movement of our age. In 2019, the first-ever UN Youth Climate Summit was held, and that same year marked the formation of Extinction Rebellion Youth (known as XRY), a group of environmental activists under the age of thirty. From local to global initiatives, young campaigners are coming together to demonstrate for action against climate change and to share visions of a fairer, safer, cleaner world. In this section, we meet the children of the climate revolution.

"WE CANNOT EAT COAL. WE CANNOT DRINK OIL."

VANESSA NAKATE

UGANDAN ACTIVIST VANESSA NAKATE IS THE FOUNDER OF THE CLIMATE ACTION GROUPS YOUTH FOR FUTURE AFRICA AND THE RISE UP MOVEMENT, WHICH AIM TO AMPLIFY THE VOICES OF AFRICAN ACTIVISTS. SHE WAS INSPIRED TO TAKE ACTION AFTER NOTICING RISING TEMPERATURES IN HER COUNTRY AND HAS CAMPAIGNED TIRELESSLY FOR CHANGE ACROSS THE CONTINENT, INCLUDING FOR THE PROTECTION OF THE CONGO RAIN FOREST.

> "THE EYES OF ALL FUTURE GENERATIONS ARE UPON YOU."

GRETA THUNBERG

Swedish teenager Greta Thunberg made headlines around the world in 2018 when she kick-started the School Strike for Climate movement, encouraging schoolchildren to miss Friday classes to protest government inaction around climate change. What began as Greta sitting alone outside the Swedish parliament grew into a global phenomenon, with an estimated 1.4 million young people from 128 countries participating.

"PEOPLE DON'T LIKE TO LISTEN TO WHAT OTHERS ARE SAYING. BUT IF YOU LOOK AT A VISUAL PIECE, HEAR MUSIC, OR EXPERIENCE . . . ARTWORK, THEY CONTAIN SYMBOLS AND MESSAGES THAT ARE UNIVERSAL."

NADIA NAZAR

Nadia Nazar is the cofounder and art director of Zero Hour, a youth-led organization that shares the voices of young people in discussions around climate and environmental justice. At fifteen, Nadia helped to design the Zero Hour logo, which works as a visual tool to help unite people of all ages and backgrounds.

"CHANGE RARELY HAPPENS FROM THE TOP DOWN. IT HAPPENS WHEN MILLIONS OF PEOPLE DEMAND CHANGE."

BRUNO RODRIGUEZ

TEEN ACTIVIST BRUNO RODRIGUEZ WAS INSPIRED TO TAKE ACTION AGAINST CLIMATE CHANGE AFTER SEEING PROTESTS ERUPTING IN EUROPE AND WANTING TO REPLICATE SIMILAR ACTIONS IN HIS HOME COUNTRY OF ARGENTINA. HE HAS SINCE GONE ON TO SET UP THE YOUTH FOR CLIMATE ARGENTINA GROUP AND WAS INVITED TO PARTICIPATE IN THE FIRST UN YOUTH CLIMATE SUMMIT. HE HOPES TO RAISE AWARENESS OF THE CLIMATE CRISIS THROUGHOUT LATIN AMERICA.

"WE MUST STOP TALKING AND TAKE ACTION."

HELENA GUALINGA

HELENA GUALINGA IS AN INDIGENOUS ENVIRONMENTALIST AND HUMAN RIGHTS ACTIVIST FROM ECUADOR. HER WORK AIMS TO AMPLIFY THE VOICES OF INDIGENOUS PEOPLE WHO ARE AT RISK OF LOSING THEIR HOMES AND WAYS OF LIFE BECAUSE OF BOTH CLIMATE CHANGE AND EXTRACTIVE INDUSTRIES DESTROYING THE LAND. IN 2020, SHE FOUNDED THE ORGANIZATION POLLUTERS OUT, WHICH AIMS TO DIMINISH THE FOSSIL FUEL INDUSTRY'S INFLUENCE AND INCORPORATE PROTECTIONS OF INDIGENOUS RIGHTS INTO THE PARIS AGREEMENT, A LEGALLY BINDING INTERNATIONAL TREATY ON CLIMATE CHANGE.

TRY THIS:

1. **Organize a flash mob.**
Gather friends to join you to create a dance, skit, or theatrical performance in public. (Be sure not to do anything that would get you in trouble.)

2. **Create a unique name and symbol for your cause.** Research symbols that have been used to represent protests and social movements. Sketch and design a symbol that relates to your social cause and conveys what you stand for. Explore adding colors to the symbol that represent its themes and values.

3. **Wear your cause.**
Fashion can be an easy form of artistic expression to wear to protests and in public. Paint a T-shirt with a protest message that shares your vision for positive change.

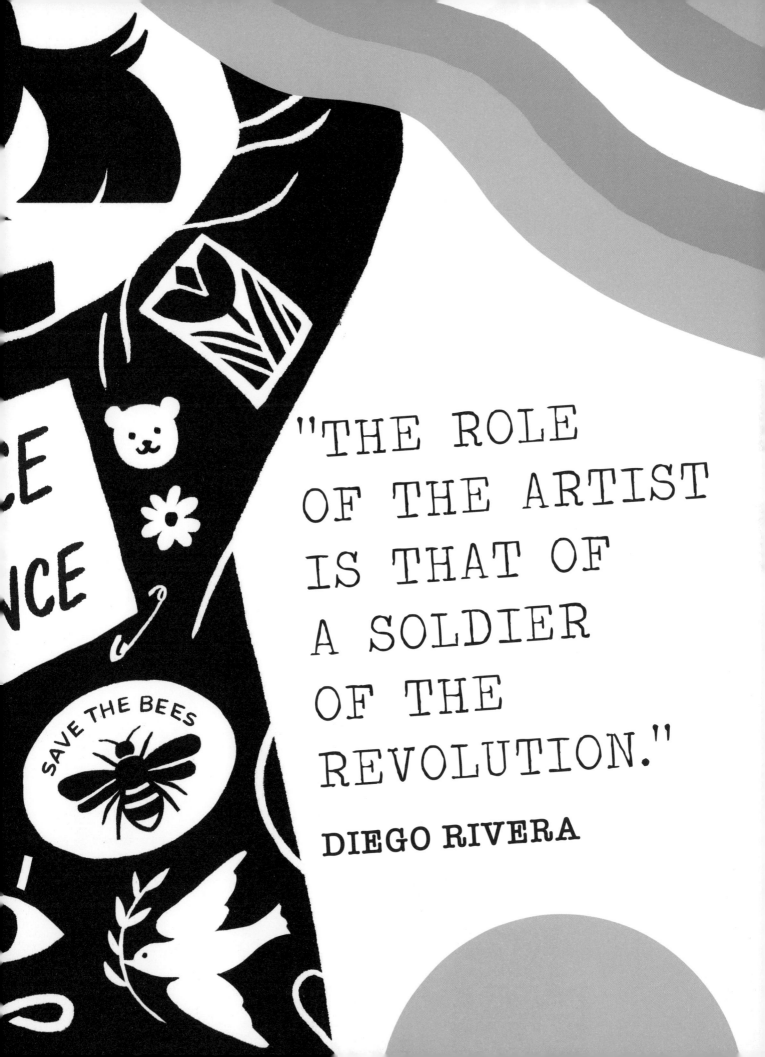

"THE ROLE
OF THE ARTIST
IS THAT OF
A SOLDIER
OF THE
REVOLUTION."

DIEGO RIVERA

04 PROTEST ART BEYOND TODAY

WHAT LIES AHEAD

With the increase, frequency, and urgent intensity of social challenges, protest art will continue to make an impact in social movements. The continuous rise of new technologies will expand these voices into digital and virtual spaces. Within the upcoming years, one might expect to see artists experiment more with existing protest art practices while integrating more video projection, augmented reality, meme development, and Internet of things (IoT). And with the vast changes that technology could bring, one might also predict that tech-based protest art will be balanced with artists choosing to create smaller, more personal protest works. Through such micro-protests, people can take everyday household items—from sticky notes to apparel, cardboard, and crafts—to creatively protest injustices and challenges that exist in their communities.

TECHNOLOGY AND PROTEST ART

Deepfakes

Deepfakes are a type of image manipulation used in social media that replaces one person's face with another's in still or video images. Deepfakes might, for instance, use celebrities' or politicians' images to mock their words or personalities, to warn of the harms and dangers that leaders have caused, and to shock viewers into changing their opinions of the public figures portrayed.

Social Media Filters

An easy and accessible way to show your support for a social movement or cause is to use a filter on your social media profile picture. Filters are made available as portable network graphic (PNG) files and can be overlaid onto any other image as a marker of affinity, to show solidarity, express your values, and build community.

Augmented Reality

Smartphones and social media have enabled us to document our lives in numerous accessible ways. Now the technology of augmented reality (AR) provides us with a new twist: the ability to superimpose images, videos, and experiences onto real-world environments. Viewers can then hold up their smartphones over the space and see a virtual world full of possibilities and experiences.

An early example of AR protesting occurred during the 2011 Occupy Wall Street actions against economic inequality in the United States. The artist Mark Skwarek rebuilt the Occupy Wall Street protests as a virtual protest space that placed photos of protesters from New York's Zuccotti Park into spaces like the New York Stock Exchange that had actually been restricted from access.

In 2020, global protests for racial justice fostered an increased removal and dismantling of monuments dedicated to abusive public figures. AR has emerged as a tool for reimagining the figures who could be put onto bases of the monuments that remain. The Movers and Shakers team in New York City uses AR to create virtual monuments to activists like athletes Colin Kaepernick and Jackie Robinson that are installed in spaces like train cars and outdoor pavilions. The artist Sebastian Errazuriz has used AR to "graffiti-bomb" and place his artworks on sculptures via social media. In 2017, the social media platform Snapchat collaborated with the artist Jeff Koons to showcase his Balloon Dog sculptures in spaces around the world. Errazuriz used technology to re-create the sculptures covered in graffiti as a "symbolic stance against an imminent AR corporate invasion."

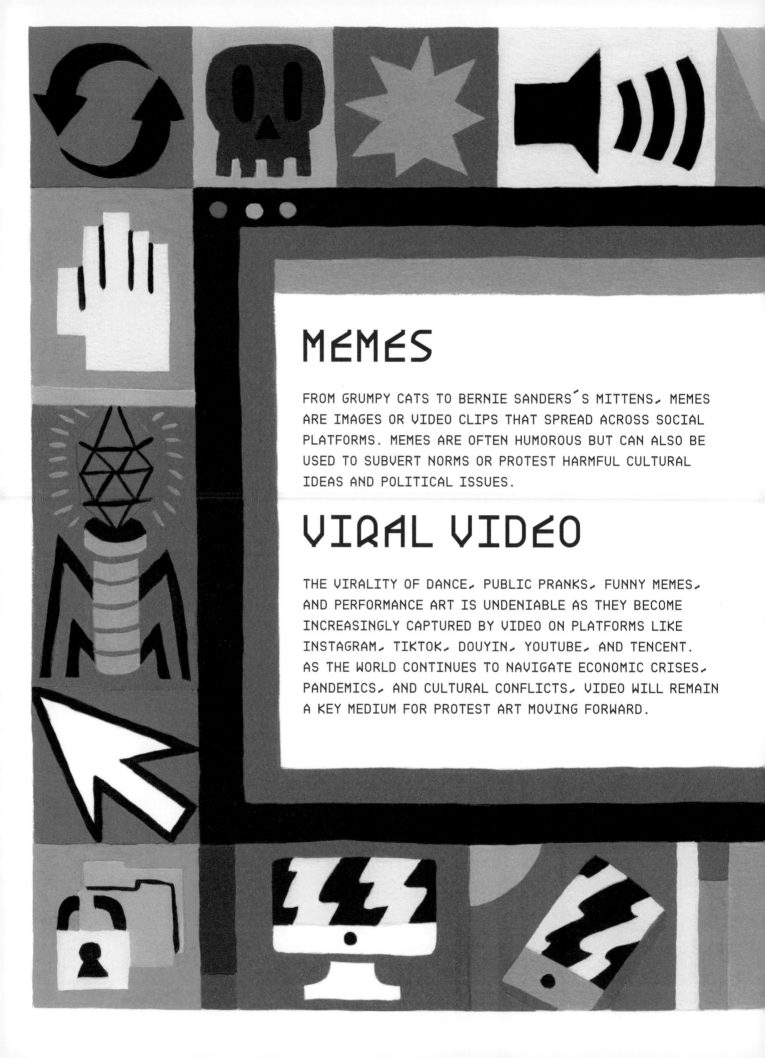

MEMES

FROM GRUMPY CATS TO BERNIE SANDERS'S MITTENS, MEMES ARE IMAGES OR VIDEO CLIPS THAT SPREAD ACROSS SOCIAL PLATFORMS. MEMES ARE OFTEN HUMOROUS BUT CAN ALSO BE USED TO SUBVERT NORMS OR PROTEST HARMFUL CULTURAL IDEAS AND POLITICAL ISSUES.

VIRAL VIDEO

THE VIRALITY OF DANCE, PUBLIC PRANKS, FUNNY MEMES, AND PERFORMANCE ART IS UNDENIABLE AS THEY BECOME INCREASINGLY CAPTURED BY VIDEO ON PLATFORMS LIKE INSTAGRAM, TIKTOK, DOUYIN, YOUTUBE, AND TENCENT. AS THE WORLD CONTINUES TO NAVIGATE ECONOMIC CRISES, PANDEMICS, AND CULTURAL CONFLICTS, VIDEO WILL REMAIN A KEY MEDIUM FOR PROTEST ART MOVING FORWARD.

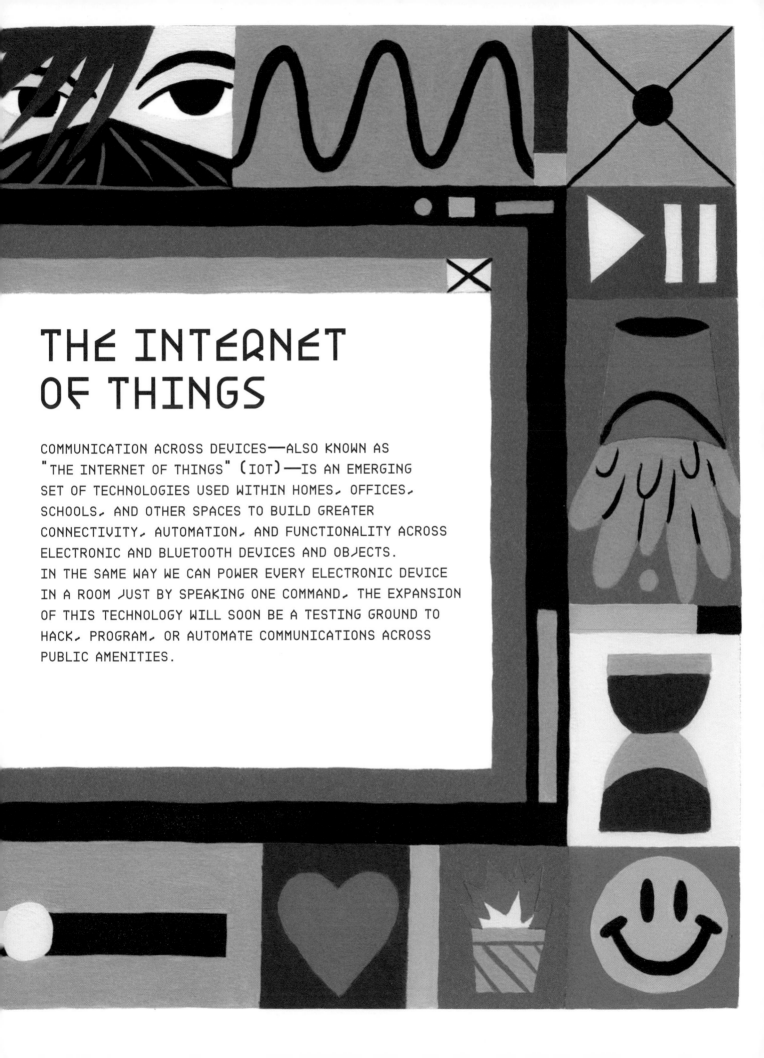

THE INTERNET OF THINGS

COMMUNICATION ACROSS DEVICES—ALSO KNOWN AS
"THE INTERNET OF THINGS" (IOT)—IS AN EMERGING
SET OF TECHNOLOGIES USED WITHIN HOMES, OFFICES,
SCHOOLS, AND OTHER SPACES TO BUILD GREATER
CONNECTIVITY, AUTOMATION, AND FUNCTIONALITY ACROSS
ELECTRONIC AND BLUETOOTH DEVICES AND OBJECTS.
IN THE SAME WAY WE CAN POWER EVERY ELECTRONIC DEVICE
IN A ROOM JUST BY SPEAKING ONE COMMAND, THE EXPANSION
OF THIS TECHNOLOGY WILL SOON BE A TESTING GROUND TO
HACK, PROGRAM, OR AUTOMATE COMMUNICATIONS ACROSS
PUBLIC AMENITIES.

M I C R O

PROTEST

In addition to high-tech efforts and long-term protest campaigns, personal and daily expressions of social resistance remain as important as ever. As an arts organizer in Ferguson in 2014, I developed a project called *Sticky Note to Self*, which became one of the most prophetic and meaningful projects I have created while also being the simplest and most personal. As a designer, I'd always been a fan of sticky notes to help me organize my thoughts. Then after falling victim to online harassment and trolling for my activism, I wrote a note to myself that reminded me to "Always do right by people," even when they were mean-spirited toward me.

On April 1, 2015, I posted that note online, and because of the wave of love and support I received in response, posting reflective notes became a semi-daily practice. The notes have covered topics of love and loss, advocated for police reform, encouraged mindfulness practices, and simply served as a way to exhale the anger and frustration I feel about various issues. As others engaged with the notes, I developed a community around their content by creating apparel, making art, and starting a YouTube series. Some of my notes have even been used by libraries and schools to teach visual art therapy and reflective writing to children and families.

I continue to be blown away by how such a small and simple canvas can lead to such an expansive set of outputs. And I think that's exactly the power of micro-protests. They demonstrate that protest does not require a grandiose undertaking. Its form can be as simple and personal as you desire. It can be a singular experience, or it can be frequent and continuous. And even though it might be small in scale, it can resound throughout a community like the ripple effects of one drop of water in a lake.

CHALK

Chalk Riot, led by artist Chelsea Ritter-Soronen, is a global community of chalk artists taking over sidewalks and walls across America, Australia, and the UK. In addition to inspirational works that spark joy and whimsy for viewers, chalk art inspires communities toward civic participation, political activism, and racial allyship. One of the appeals of chalk as a medium for protest art is that it is ephemeral, so there is more general openness to its use over paint or more permanent media.

ZINES

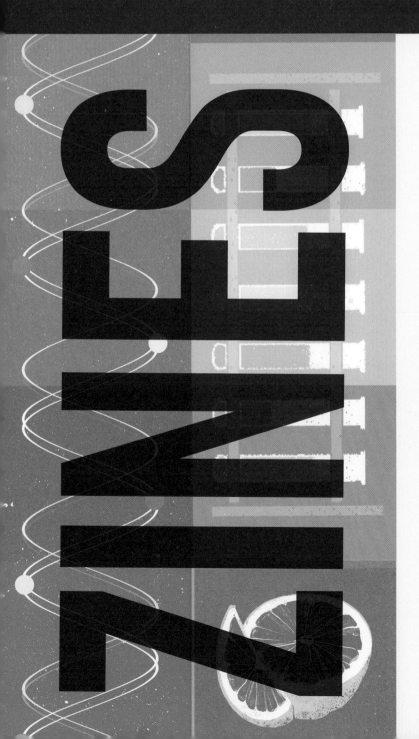

When I was a kid, I would often make tiny folded and stapled booklets that contained stories or my thoughts on a topic along with doodles and images collaged from my mother's magazines. I kept my booklet collection on my bookshelf, but sometimes I was so proud of what I produced that I would share my favorites with friends at school. It wasn't until college that I learned that my booklets were an art form known as zines.

Handmade or small-run pamphlets date back to the 1700s, when writers published their opinions on political events of the day. A famous example is Thomas Paine's *Common Sense*, which advocated for American independence from Great Britain.

Zines take their name from the term *fanzine* (a combination of the words *fan* and *magazine*) and were originally created to express an individual's or group's interest in a specific topic. They can be handwritten, collaged, photocopied, or produced in digital form. In protest movements, zines have been a helpful tool for distributing news and information, inspiring change and action, teaching a skill, educating people on a complex topic, or documenting actions.

TRY THIS:

1. **Make a video** that expresses your opinion and viewpoint on a topic that matters to you. Share it with a circle of friends and ask them to respond to it and/or amplify it. And if you're feeling bold, share it more widely to start a conversation with others.

2. **Create a meme!** Find an image, video, or GIF that is compelling or comical to you. Reinterpret it as a protest message by adding text that expresses an action people can take to help a social justice cause you care about. Share it with friends on your favorite social media platform and engage them in conversation about the topic.

3. **Design your own protest zine.** Share your thoughts on a topic by making a short booklet about it. You can either use one sheet of paper folded to create multiple pages or cut, fold, and nest multiple sheets.

Use markers and pens to write or draw content on each page. Collage images from magazines to help illustrate your thoughts. Once it's complete, make multiple copies of your zine and use a stapler to bind the pages together. If you feel bold, leave copies in random places for others to find and read.

"ARTMAKING IS MAKING THE *invisible,* **VISIBLE."**

—MARCEL DUCHAMP

OVER TO YOU

Our world right now is ripe for change, for progress, and for new ideas of what tomorrow can bring.

As we continue to fight for racial justice, environmental sustainability, economic fairness, LGBTQ+ rights, public health, and so much more, our collective well-being depends on people rising up with vision, leadership, and unity to demand more of our existing systems and set a solid path forward to unlock new possibilities. I believe that artists are those visionaries, and I believe in the voice and collective power of protesters and activists to steer us on this hopeful journey. As you have read the stories, witnessed the artworks, and learned the skills shared in this book, it is my deepest desire that you have been equipped and inspired to become a creative warrior—an artivist—in your community. I hope that you have been guided in identifying the causes you care about and sharpening your creative muscles to take action through artmaking. And, finally—if nothing else—I hope this book has helped you understand and believe in the power of art as protest.

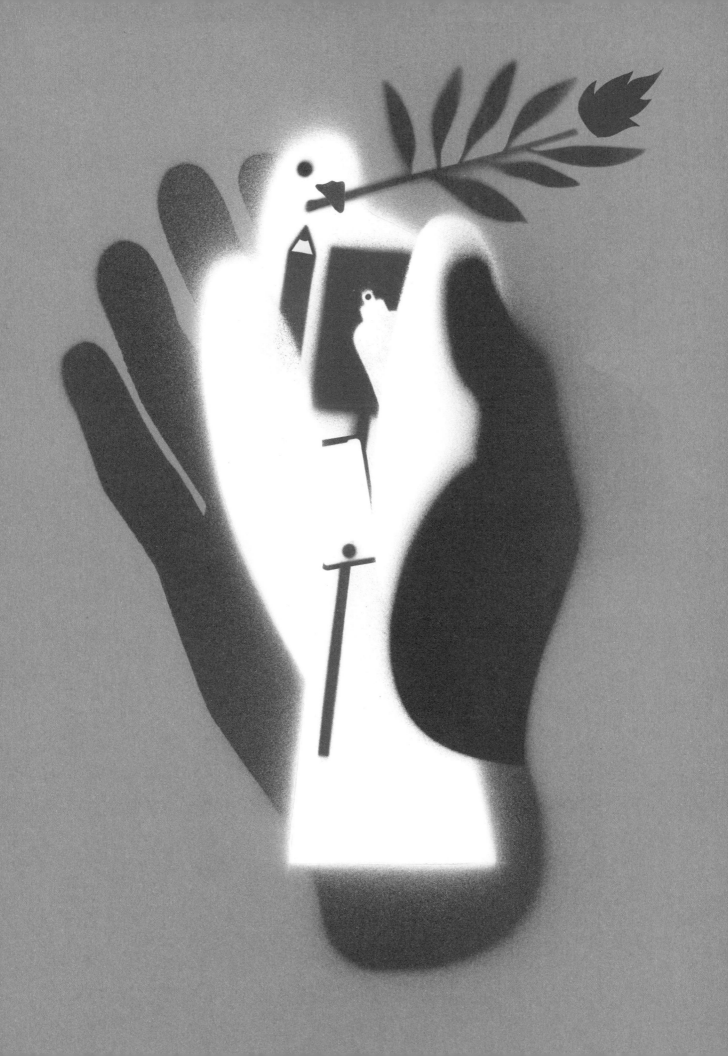

MEET THE

DE NICHOLS

De Nichols is an arts-based organizer, social impact designer, social entrepreneur, and keynote lecturer. She currently works as a senior user experience researcher of product inclusion at YouTube and as a core organizer of the global collective Design as Protest. She previously served as the principal of design and social practice at Civic Creatives, a design strategy agency she created in St. Louis. One of her most famous and influential works, the *Mirror Casket*, was cited in an article by Angela Davis entitled "The Art of Protest."

DIANA DAGADITA

Diana Dagadita is a graduate of Solent University, in the UK, with a BA in illustration. They are a freelance illustrator and printmaker currently living in London. Their first book, *Printer's ABC*, was published in 2019.

MOLLY MENDOZA

Molly Mendoza is an illustrator currently living in Portland, Oregon. She is a BFA graduate from the Pacific Northwest College of Art and recipient of the RockStar Games Award from the 2015 SOI Student Competition. Her clients have included Adobe, the *New York Times,* and *The Scientist* magazine. Her first graphic novel, *Skip*, was published in 2019 to critical acclaim.

CREATORS

OLIVIA TWIST

Olivia Twist is a London-based illustrator, arts facilitator, and lecturer who graduated from the Royal College of Art in the UK with an MA in visual communication. She is a winner of the Quentin Blake Narrative Drawing Prize and was included in Taschen's 2019 *Best 100 Illustrators from Around the World*. Her commissions and clients include the Wellcome Collection and WeTransfer.

SADDO

Saddo is the pseudonym of Raul Oprea, a contemporary painter, muralist, and illustrator who has exhibited his work in galleries all over the world, including in his home country, Romania, as well as in the United States, Canada, Austria, Denmark, and El Salvador. He was the founding member of the Playground, one of Romania's first street art groups.

DIEGO BECAS

Diego Becas is an illustrator, designer, and multi-disciplinary graphic artist based in Santiago, Chile. His work has been commissioned by many publishing houses, theaters, magazines, and festivals. He uses traditional methods and materials, including engraving, cut paper, wood, ink, watercolor, acrylic, and hand-lettering, usually working with a reduced color palette.

START *MAKING.*

Start *CREATING*

THE CHANGE

that's needed

for a

BETTER WORLD.